Manifest
the Perfect
Mate

Manifest the Perfect Mate

Find the Love & Respect You Desire

Paula Langguth Ryan

MEDIA

Published 2021 by Gildan Media LLC
aka G&D Media
www.GandDmedia.com

Front cover design by David Rheinhardt of Pyrographx

Interior design by Meghan Day Healey of Story Horse, LLC

Library of Congress Cataloging-in-Publication Data is available upon request

ISBN: 978-1-7225-0564-6

10   9   8   7   6   5   4   3   2   1

Author's Note

If you are on a quest to know yourself deeper, and to break free of your fears of abandonment and unworthiness, you are holding the key to this freedom in your hands, right now. The path to drawing the Right and Perfect Mate into your life begins—and ends—with *you* becoming the person you want to have in your life, which then will be mirrored in your relationships.

When I began teaching this material two decades ago, I had no idea how much it would resonate with people worldwide. It has been an honor and a privilege to help so many people navigate their way to their heart's deepest desires.

It has also been my great pleasure to help others create more of what they want in all areas of their lives for more than a quarter century (so far!).

This book is part of the *Manifest the Right and Perfect Life* series, which includes volumes to help you bring forth the right and perfect Job, Clients, Employees, and even the right and perfect Buyer for Your Home. If there's another topic you'd like to see me include in this series, please drop me a note.

May your soul always feel its worth—and may you always source your true value from within yourself.

—Paula Langguth Ryan

———·••·———

"I thank all who have loved me in their hearts,
With thanks and love from mine."

—ELIZABETH BARRETT BROWNING

———·••·———

Contents

⌐————•••————⌐

Introduction

Can I speak candidly to you? Think of me as that trusted friend who is willing to share some hard truths with you about relationships. Whether we're in relationships or seeking relationships, all too often our thoughts center on how we can "get" love, attention, connection, a sense of security and so on.

I'm here to tell you that you're not only looking for love in all the wrong places—you're also looking for love for all the wrong reasons. (I told you I was going to be blunt!)

We're fixated, I dare say, on getting something from someone in almost all of our relationships. We want a partner who won't abandon us, who will help ease those places where we feel unsafe, unworthy, powerless, lacking and so on. I know the fear that drives these actions.

The fear is that if you honor yourself, speak your truth, or stand up for yourself, the other person will leave you, or stop dating you, or stop calling you. That's the fear. We're deeply afraid of being "lonely, lonely loners" as Sid the sloth from *Ice Age* would say.

As a result, we expend great effort trying to be who we think someone else—our mate or potential mate—wants us to be. We lose sight of *who* we are, how *we* want to show up in relationship, and what we *want* in a long-term partner.

The same goes for your intended. If you give people room to be themselves and allow them to have their feelings, and not try to fix the situation, and not close down because they're shutting down, you open up a huge opportunity to create the relationship you really want. When you close down it's because you're focusing on what you *don't* want.

As you read this book, you're going to change that. You're going to remember who you are and what you want in a relationship.

1

Focus on the Feeling

Are you looking to manifest a new relationship, or revitalize a current relationship? Either goal is within your reach if you're willing to recognize and release the fears and old stories that keep you from being fully open to love.

This book will hold great value for you, for all your relationships, provided you steadfastly do the recommended activities. Before you proceed, grab something to write with, as you'll be doing exercises that will require you to write things down.

When you are looking to manifest the right and perfect mate in your life (new or current), the first thing you need to look at is what you want the relationship to *feel* like, as opposed to what you want the relationship to *look* like.

We all get caught up in what we want our romantic relationships to look like, with all the intricate details we believe are important. And we're so focused on the external that we completely miss the internal "deal-breakers" until we're immersed in a relationship. Instead of focusing on the external appearance—if you *truly* want to draw the right and perfect mate to you—focus on what the *essence* is that you want in your life.

What do I mean by essence?

The essence of your desired relationship refers to all those inherent, indispensable qualities in a relationship that feed your soul. What do you truly desire in a mate? I want you to make a list.

It's often easier to make a list of what you *don't* want, so start there. You want a mate who doesn't do what? Who doesn't get possessive? Who doesn't put you down or make you feel small? Write it all down on your list. What don't you want a mate to be like? You want a mate who doesn't make you feel what?

Once you've made that list, look at each of the items you *don't* want and ask yourself, "What do I really want instead of this?" When you focus on what you *don't* want in a relationship, you continue to draw those qualities to you. In order to draw the right and perfect mate to you, you need to focus on what it is you *truly want* instead of these unwanted attributes.

Clarity on What I Want

What I Don't Want is . . .	What I Truly Want is . . .

For example, say your list includes this statement: "I want someone who doesn't get possessive." Write down what it is you really want regarding this aspect of your right and perfect mate: "What I really want is someone who is secure enough not to be threatened by my independence. I really want someone who truly enjoys, supports and celebrates my independence."

Or maybe your list includes: "I want someone who doesn't put me down and make me feel small." Write down what it is you really want: "What I really want is someone who is loving, supportive, mature, kind, joyful, confident."

Or maybe your list includes: "I want someone who doesn't constantly need me to be strong." Write down what you really want. "What I really want is someone who is my equal; someone who complements me."

Make a list of all the attributes that resonate for you. What are all those pieces that make up the right and perfect mate for you?

Once you make that list, set it aside. We'll get back to it in a bit.

Transform Old Relationship Issues into Gifts

Now that you've set into motion the energy of attraction for the essence of your relationship, it's time to roll up your sleeves and clean up past relationship issues.

It's time to take care of whatever you're still carrying around from your past relationships.

These include old resentments, anger, fear, regret—any and all unresolved issues. Don't think you have any of this baggage? It's time to get completely honest with yourself. Rest assured, there are still unresolved issues lurking in the dark corners of your mind, if you ever find yourself saying or even thinking things like the following:

I wouldn't be in this position if so and so hadn't done x, y or z.

I would trust people more if so and so hadn't done x, y or z.

The time has come to sit down and write a letter to every person you've ever loved or been in a relationship with. It's time to thank them for what they gave you. No matter how horrible the relationship was or how it ended, I want you to find and recognize the tangible and intangible gifts that relationship gave you. I want you to honor all the gifts that you gained from that relationship.

Here's why. The truth is, every relationship you had in the past was the right and perfect relationship for you *at that time.*

It was what you needed, wanted or desired in your life at that time. For whatever reasons. Don't beat yourself up about it. Honor that truth. Do not live in the past. Guilt from past relationships can sabotage even the healthiest relationship in your life. Guilt is a core belief that you may need to transform on a deeper level, but this letter writing exercise will get you started, by helping you recognize what still needs healing (see *Sample Letter of Thanks* at the end of this chapter).

What were the gifts you received from these previous connections? For example, some people get married or get into relationships so they can have stability and security for themselves and their (present or potential) children. The person selected may or may not have wound up being the "love of their life," yet it was the right and perfect relationship at that time. It was the companionship and security they desired then.

Other people get married or get into relationships so they can make themselves feel more important, or more powerful.

The thing to remember for yourself is this: Every relationship you've ever had has been specifically designed to bring you closer to the right and perfect relationship today. So thank *every* relationship for the gifts you gained.

How do you determine the gifts you've gained? Examine all your past relationships with a singular focus on how it helped you grow. Maybe one past relationship taught you how to stand up for yourself, how to value yourself. You finally got pushed to the brink and said, "Enough is enough," and you stood up for yourself. Thank that relationship for teaching you to honor yourself.

Or maybe a relationship taught you how to have self-respect.

Maybe one taught you how to step outside your safe box, your comfort zone. I know a lot of men who thanked the women who divorced them because they were couch potatoes. Getting divorced really shook them up, tossed them out of their box and made them explore who they really were, and what they were interested in. I want you to seek—and find—the gift in each relationship.

Write a letter to thank each person, one by one. Write the letters as if you're going to send them, or as if no one is going to ever see them. It is your choice whether or not you're sending them. The mandatory part is to write as authentically as possible. Write each of your past relationships with open and honest gratitude and thank them for those gifts. This exercise is also helpful for any current relationship you're in. Expressing gratitude for everything in your relationship so far is a great way to add new life to your current relationship.

You may also find you carry around resentments and issues from your parents, or the adults who often were your first role models of how to navigate the ins and outs of relationships. You learned a great deal about relationship dynamics—good or bad—from your parents. Write thank you letters to the people who served those roles for you.

What your parents taught you helped you become the person you are today. Thank them. Find the gifts in those relationships, no matter how much you liked or didn't like your parents, how they treated each other, how they conducted their own relationships and the way they raised you. Find the gifts they gave you with their relationship dynamics, and extend your gratitude to them with a thank you letter.

Sample Letter of Thanks

Dear _____,

Thank you for teaching me how to _____

_____

_____

_____

_____

_____

I learned _____

_____

_____

_____

_____

_____

I am grateeful for our time together.

Yours truly,

_____

2

The Most Powerful Relationship Question

How often do you get into a relationship where everything is going along smoothly and then something pushes a button where your brain immediately goes into fight or flight mode?

"Oh, here we go again. This person is just like all the other people I've dated!"

Whatever declaration of defeat pops into your head, take a minute to stop and ask yourself one simple, yet powerful, question:

Is this situation, whatever is going on right now, really about this person, or is this a projection I'm putting on this person from my past?

The more intense your reaction to something that's happening now, the greater likelihood you're projecting.

Whenever you find yourself wanting to run from a relationship (whether old or new!), or compiling a list of "annoying, negative traits" you don't like about the person, the simple, yet powerful question above is something you *must* learn to ask yourself if you want to break old relationship patterns.

Let's say you had a past relationship with an alcoholic. You find yourself dating someone new, and one night you're out to dinner and the person has two or three drinks. Do you immediately assume the person is like your old alcoholic ex? Just because they had a couple of drinks doesn't necessarily mean they are an alcoholic. It's simply reminding you of that situation. Be ready to bring that up in conversation, and state the microscopic truth of what's coming up for you.

It can be as simple as saying, "I'm having a little challenge right now, this evening. You having a couple of drinks is reminding me of a past relationship and the issues that came up because the person I was dating was an alcoholic."

Addressing the elephant in the room directly is the single best way to create fully authentic and communicative relationships. I understand that having this awareness and this conversation in the moment may not be possible just yet. In that case, sit yourself down alone after the event and recognize for yourself what happened within you. "I imagined the situation that happened this evening was actually my old alcoholic ex. This isn't that person at all. This is a new person and I was merely projecting my old fears about the way alcohol has affected my past relationships."

Maybe old issues around abandonment or unworthiness come to mind. Whatever comes up, be 100% honest and authentic about what's coming up for you, and own whatever it is you are projecting onto this person. Check in with yourself to see whether this is a projection or not.

A big clue that it *is* a projection is when the *old* person comes into mind during the situation. Is this a justifiable red flag and deal-breaker, or is it simply a fear coming up? Is this person the one who has a problem or are *you* simply afraid of repeating an old pattern that really doesn't have any foundation in this situation?

If this is just a fear, take a minute and see this new person in front of you as loving, kind and compassionate. See them open, passionate, patient; see them communicative, trusting, secure, positive, energized, healthy, happy and mature (that's always a big one).

For a relationship you are desiring, or a relationship you are currently in, the next thing I want you to do is visualize the attributes you want your mate to have. Pay close attention to where your old baggage and hidden beliefs or emotions try and guide you to adding attributes to the list that are aspects of yourself you don't like.

Truly assess the differences you see between you and the other person. Can you be with these differences without running? Can you stay present while this person navigates *their* shadows, or are you too afraid of your own darkness to sit with and hold space as they heal their woundedness, in the same ways you would want them to do for you?

Whatever attributes you are suddenly seeing as lacking in another may actually be a projection of something from a past relationship. See the person in front of you as being infused with the positive attributes instead of the projected ones. You might even remind yourself: "This is a whole different person; this is not my ex."

Then release your expectations of the form this relationship is going to take. You might even remind yourself, "This is a projection!" It may indeed be something you've done before. You need to watch for that— *and* not make it the truth about *this* relationship, based on a single interaction.

Take a minute to reflect on what's coming up for you. Am I going down an old road again? Is this an old pattern I'm repeating? Be honest with yourself. Do I need to walk away from this? Is this not right for me? Or is this just my old fear getting in the way of something that could be really good?

When an old pattern pops up in an existing relationship ask yourself what you can do differently to honor yourself. By recognizing and verbalizing where you're being triggered by—and possibly are reacting to—an old pattern, you begin to break the pattern.

You could even go so far as to say, "Hey, I know you're not so-and-so. But what just happened triggered an old memory with that person and I need a minute to work through that so I can be fully present to you." And you can support your partner when *they* get triggered, by lovingly saying, "You know, I'm not so-and-so."

If a fear comes up for you, acknowledge that it's okay to let go of someone. You don't have to stay in a relationship or continue dating someone, simply because you're afraid of being alone. That small acknowledgment may be all that's needed to give yourself permission to observe and explore these old patterns of projection.

The path to finding the right and perfect mate revolves around creating the energy that's going to draw the right and perfect mate to you. You may date some people who aren't the right and perfect mate for you long-term. But they may be the right and perfect mate for you right now, while you work through some of the relationship issues you may still be carrying around with you.

Rekindle Relationship Attributes You're Missing

Are there certain attributes that were once present in a relationship you want to rekindle? If so, there's one more action you can take.

When a behavior appears in your relationship that you don't want, avoid affirming to yourself, "There he or she goes again."

Instead, ask yourself—going back to your list—*what do I really want*? If you really want to be with this person, then see him or her the way you want them to be. People conform to our expectations all the time. They either rise to that level or they fall to that level, whatever we expected.

Mind you, I'm not saying that it's someone else's responsibility to make us happy. What I'm talking about here is paying attention to where you have a built-in expectation that someone else's behavior is going to be something unacceptable. Those places where you've already decided that they are triggering you in a negative way, creating an emotional response that, in hindsight, appears overblown for the circumstances that occurred. Those places where you're making assumptions and assigning meaning. (We will explore expectations versus expectancies a bit later.)

If you're in a relationship and you believe it is the right and perfect relationship, but it's needing some dynamic changes, it's up to you to change (in your mind) the way you're holding that relationship. The key is to look at and talk about how you *experience* the behavior, not to blame or attack your partner. Usually, our go-to response is, "Hey when you did this, I felt unsafe. So you need to stop that!" In other words, you want the other person to change *their* behavior so *you* will feel better. That's a recipe for disaster.

My friend Ryan beautifully points out that "prayer and meditation, when used frequently and honestly, are the healing balm to all irritations." Let me share with you how he and his partner, Emily, pray together:

How do you pray with a partner? It's easy. "Hey God, it's me, Ryan. I have been feeling very irritated with Emily lately and judging some of her behaviors. I feel like it's getting in the way of me being able to love her unconditionally and I can't see clearly what my part of the situation is aside from that. Am I projecting? Being selfish? Living from social conditioning? I can't tell anymore. Can You help me to see clearly what is going on and help what's in me that needs healing? And with that I will pass to Emily.

"God, it's Emily. I didn't know Ryan felt that way and I am not sure how to proceed. I want to be with him but I am afraid that if I change too much of myself I will become codependent in this relationship and live out old patterns. Can You help me to heal and move forward in a way that is healthy for both of us? Amen."

Then we sit in the quiet together and wait for the healing and peace to happen. Sometimes more discussions need to take place as we have built thick defense mechanisms around our hearts to protect ourselves from getting hurt.

Ryan's ultimate "mic-drop" advice: Be patient with each other.

3

Keep Your Mind, Words and Actions Focused

Sometimes, especially if you're in a long-term relationship that seems to have soured, it's necessary to consciously redirect your thoughts, words and actions. This chapter will help you do so. I warn you, though: This may not be the most pleasant chapter to read. It is, however, probably the most important.

My manifesting mentor, Rev. Catherine Ponder, tells a wonderful story about a woman who was married for many years. This story may at first glance scare you more than it inspires you. Pay attention to what fears and memories get triggered for you. What core beliefs—abandonment, unworthiness, powerlessness, lack/limitation, guilt, or death and dying off—come to the surface? You may be tempted to shut down or avoid these beliefs. Please don't. I encourage you to stay with the feelings. Stop reading this book if you need to and sit quiet with the emotions that wash over you. Healing these parts will move you forward exponentially toward having healthier relationships. I guarantee it. Here is the story just as Catherine Ponder related.

Every night after dinner, the woman and her husband would sit in front of the fire in their easy chairs and they would read to each other and it was very lovely for them. Then all of a sudden, the husband started not coming home, or he would come home for dinner and then leave again to go back to the office.

She found out he was having an affair with someone from his office. Instead of being passive-aggressive, or confronting him and getting angry, or getting defensive and feeling hurt, what she did was to sit down and ask herself, "What do I really want? Do I want to leave him? Do I want to divorce him? Or do I want to have the relationship we previously had?"

She asked herself these questions to get clear about what it was *she* really wanted. She realized she truly wanted to continue to have a relationship with her husband. She wanted it to be a strong, vibrant relationship where they sat in their easy chairs at night after dinner and read to each other.

She started consciously holding in her mind what she truly wanted. Not with just a repetitive mantra or affirmation, but with her actions. With her thoughts.

After dinner, when he left each night to go to the office to "work," she started sitting in her easy chair, next to his easy chair and she would read aloud as if he *was* there. She sat there and held that space for him night after night after night.

A couple of weeks went by, and every night she sat there, seeing her relationship how she wanted it to be, seeing what she truly desired.

That's what you need to focus on—seeing what you want—as hard as it is at times.

One day he pushed himself back from the table and said, "I've decided to stay home tonight." He stayed home, they read together, and they had a great time.

Then, another night, he pushed himself away from the dinner table and left again. It would have been very easy for his wife to throw up her hands and say, "Forget it! This isn't going to work! I can't do this alone!" But she didn't do that. She stayed focused on what she desired. She knew this wasn't the end of their relationship and she decided to actively engage in healing the relationship without anger or fear. This is not always the easiest path to take, unless you're willing to heal your own unhealed relationship issues, as I outlined in Chapter 2.

Remember, relationships are not always 50%–50%. Sometimes they're 70%–30% or 30%–70%, or 90%–10% or 10%–90%. Relationships flow. They're part of the ebb and flow of energy. Stay the course, just as this woman did, if you believe your relationship is one worth continuing.

After her husband left that next evening, she took up her position as if he were there. A few more weeks went by, and she held this space, until he once again pushed back his chair and declared he was going to stay home that night.

The next night he left. A few more days went by with him leaving. She continued to read in front of the fire by herself, always holding that space. Then one night, he stayed home again. The next night he left again. A few more days went by, and he again stayed home, and never left again after dinner to go to "work."

How did this happen? Instead of getting upset about what it was she *didn't* want, she focused on what she *did* want. She kept holding that space. This is not about having discipline, or the will power to hold space. This is not about having an angelic mindset. This is about staying clearly focused on what you truly desire. We will get back to this story a little later. For now, do the following exercise with great courage.

Exercise: Make a fearless inventory of everything that got triggered as you read the above story. Write it all down. Look at what hurts. Talk it through with a professional. These core beliefs that get triggered are the guiding lights that show us where we abandon ourselves, give away our power, de-value ourselves, belittle ourselves, and so on.

Once you've had time to reflect on your deeper healing work, it's time to get microscopically honest about what you truly desire when a conflict arises in your relationship. Do you want to engage in a fight with your beloved? Or do you want to heal the relationship you have? The choice is *entirely* yours!

4

Become the Partner You Want In Your Life

Let's go back to the *Clarity on What I Want* list that you created in Chapter 1, where you wrote down the essence of what you want in your life.

Take that list out and look at it long and hard and—most importantly—honestly. Circle any attributes on your list you want in a right and perfect mate which you are not displaying yourself.

Do you have patient, loving, or supportive as attributes on your list? If so, then you need to ask yourself some follow-up questions: "Where am I not being patient? Where am I not being loving? Where am I not being supportive?" Anywhere in your life—not just in this relationship—where are *you* not being the essence of what you want? Where are *you* not being confident? Where are *you* not being secure? Where are *you* not being respectful? Especially to *yourself*.

Now's the time to begin to create the life you desire *with yourself*. When you do, the life you desire with a partner will manifest. The change comes from the inside to the outside. What you project when you love yourself becomes a magnetic force that demonstrates how other people are to love you. How other people will treat you. It all starts with how we treat ourselves and what we truly want.

Too often, we put off doing things we want to do because we are waiting for someone to come along and do them with us, or even *for* us, because we don't like our own company—we don't feel complete by ourselves, or we don't truly love ourselves.

For example, I once met a woman who, at the age of forty, was waiting to travel and do things she really wanted to do, because she was waiting for the right and perfect mate to come along with her.

She finally decided she would go out and do some of those things that she'd always wanted to do. She wasn't going to wait another year to do it with someone who was going to be the right and perfect mate. She decided she was going to travel by herself, or she would take a friend with her.

If you're waiting to do something with a partner or waiting to travel, or anything else, ask yourself, "Where do I want to go? What do I want to do?" If you like going to dinner theater, for example, and you don't have anyone to go with you, then simply go by yourself to the local dinner theater. Go see a movie. Go to a concert. Go wander through the art gallery. Start to do the things that resonate with *you*.

Ask a friend if you want, but, in the end, don't delay doing what you dream of doing because you're waiting for someone to join you. Begin today to live the life you truly desire. That's how the right and perfect mate is going to manifest.

Now, let's look at what else may be getting in the way of you finding your right and perfect mate, starting with the internal walls we have put up to safeguard ourselves from having our hearts broken.

5

Eliminate the Obstacles to Having Your Right and Perfect Mate

Do you ever feel like you'll *never* meet anybody you're attracted to? Ever find yourself thinking you're stuck in a rut in your relationship, and that nothing will ever change so you might as well just call it quits? Watch the language you use. If you say things like, "Oh, I'll never meet anybody," or, "this person is never going to change," remember: NEVER is a powerful word. A very powerful word.

Watch Your Language

Once you write down the essence of what you want in a mate, stop affirming that you will *never* find someone who is attractive to you—or that's exactly what is going to happen.

Stop affirming that no one you date winds up actually being someone you want to be in a relationship with. Every time you affirm statements like that, you make it a very real statement.

"I never meet anyone I'm attracted to." Think about that. If you keep affirming this, what exactly do you think is going to happen? You are never going to meet anyone you are attracted to. Is that really what you want right now? If so, that's okay. Acknowledge that. There is nothing wrong with saying, "Right now, I'd rather curl up on the couch or in bed with a good book than with anyone else." Ask yourself honestly what is it you want. And then honor that.

But if you do choose that you want the right and perfect mate right now, do not affirm, "I'm never going to meet anyone that I'm attracted to." Instead, reverse the statement. Start affirming things like:

> *I see myself easily and effortlessly drawing to me people I'm attracted to and who are attracted to me.*

> *I see myself easily and effortlessly running into people I'm attracted to, who are attracted to me.*

I see myself easily and effortlessly interacting with people I'm attracted to and who are attracted to me.

I see myself easily and effortlessly going on a date with someone I'm attracted to and who is attracted to me.

I see myself comfortably enjoying a relationship with someone I'm attracted to, and who is attracted to me.

Have you *ever* in your life met someone you were attracted to? No matter how long ago it was. I don't care if it was 50 years ago. If you have, then it is *possible* you can meet someone you're attracted to and it is possible that your current mate (and you) *can* change the relationship pattern you've setup. So, never say, "Never," because using the word *never* isn't actually accurate.

A few years ago, a woman I counseled told me that my work had saved her marriage. She had come to me nearly two decades earlier ready to walk away from her marriage. "We just don't have anything in common anymore," she told me. I replied, "You have two small children together, don't you? You have that in common."

Armed with that truth, she was able to move out of the "never/nothing" pattern of thinking and move into the place of possibilities. To this day they are still happily married.

Here are two other opposite-spectrum couples who are still together after decades of marriage.

When I was a teenager, I attended an environmental camp for several years. My camp counselor, Joni, was married to a nuclear engineer. When they were newly married, Joni was part of the environmental protesters who chanted outside the local nuclear power plant gates every morning. The very plant where her husband worked the night shift.

When he came walking out the gate after his shift, she'd be waiting for him. She'd get out of the car, kiss him, hand him the car keys and pull her protest sign out of the back seat. In the evening, he'd return, put her sign in the back seat for her, hand her the car keys and kiss her goodnight before heading in to work.

And then there's the legendary marriage of James Carville (a prominent Democratic strategist) who met his wife, Republican (now Libertarian) political consultant Mary Matalin in 1992 when they were working, respectively, on the Bill Clinton and George H.W. Bush presidential campaigns. It was love at first sight. As Matalin says, "Love is blind; love is deaf" when it comes to our beliefs.

They married in 1993, a year after they met, on Thanksgiving Day. The secret to their successful marriage: They do not talk politics at home.

Attraction, and love, happen whenever and wherever two people are open to the possibility. You have to be willing to fan and nurture the spark of attraction and the flame of love.

Fan the Spark of Attraction

Ask yourself, "Do I *believe* I can meet someone I'm attracted to? Do I believe I can rekindle the spark in the relationship I'm in?"

You have to believe it.

"Am I *ready* to meet someone I'm attracted to? Am I ready to revitalize my existing relationship?"

If you want to meet someone you're attracted to or renew the romance in your existing relationship, then you have to feel attractive to yourself. The most attractive attribute any person can have is self-confidence.

If you don't feel attractive, ask yourself, "What do I want to do to *feel* more attractive?" Not for someone else—just for *you*. You have to love yourself the way you want to be loved by another. The truth is, no one can love you more than you love yourself. The way you treat yourself is the guideline people use when they treat you. Ever feel "disrespected" by others? Who disrespects you the most? Ever feel abandoned or unworthy? Who abandons and devalues you the most? I guarantee it's a short list, with your name at the top.

Exercise: Make a list—a bucket list for every day hopes and desires. Use the *Building My Everyday Bucket List* worksheet at the end of this chapter as an example and start filling in your list now. Maybe you think you need to lose or gain weight. If that's the case, get clear about your target weight. Don't be vague. Be very concrete. Maybe you want to shed or release 20 or 30 pounds. I encourage you to avoid the word "lose"—because when we lose something, subconsciously, we're always trying to "find it" again!

Do you like exercising? Where can you go for an exercise class? Put down on your bucket list "find and call a gym that offers low-impact workouts."

Do you like dancing? Find a studio that offers dance lessons where you don't need to bring a partner with you. Do you like yoga? Seek out classes where potential partners might be. When my beloved and I go dancing, we often run into a gentleman we call "dancing guy." He comes and dances by himself, and his t-shirt says "Dancing is my Rx."

Do you like walking? Get involved with the Sierra Club, go hiking, or join a local hiking Meet-Up group.

Once *you* see yourself as attractive, worthy of and willing to do the things you love to do, then other people will be attracted to that self-confidence. Other people simply mirror what it is you see about yourself.

Building My Everyday Bucket List

Today I want to focus my attention on _____

_____

_____

_____

_____

Ten ways or places I can be

doing something toward this goal:

1. _____
2. _____
3. _____
4. _____
5. _____
6. _____
7. _____
8. _____
9. _____
10. _____

Activities that make me feel _____:

_____

_____

_____

_____

Now, it's time to look at what happens when we actually reach out and make ourselves vulnerable by actively engaging romantically with someone we think we might enjoy sharing time with.

6

Release Your Expectations

Ready to possibly, maybe, think about having a "date" with someone? Then, I've got some questions for you.

What's your biggest fear when you go on a new date, or you think about connecting romantically with your existing mate?

Most people say their biggest fear about a new date is that there will be no spark or that they'll be rejected.

The truth is, there's an even bigger fear that people don't like to admit—it is insidious—and it can blindside you.

Our biggest fear is that something about the person you are spending time with won't live up to an expectation that you have.

In the past, you may have been disappointed by someone (or even this current person). We say things like, "I always find there's no spark, or it's been disappointing in some way."

Instead, affirm that this is now behind you. Say, "In the past, I've been disappointed. From this moment on, I know that everyone I meet is exactly who they say they are, despite any appearances to the contrary."

Can you believe that statement? If not, ask yourself, "Why can't I believe that?"

If you can't believe that everyone you meet is exactly who they say they are despite any appearances to the contrary, what you're doing is filtering this new experience through the lens of past experiences. Where don't you "trust" them? Or, more importantly, where don't you trust *yourself*?

It always comes back to the past. If you're using an internet dating site for example, maybe someone's pictures don't quite match up to real life.

Is a picture really that important? Those of you who have seen pictures of me know that I've had many different looks in my career. Some were more attractive than others. (I'm thinking specifically of my college freshman "perm gone wrong" as I write this!) Some would be more compelling to one person than another.

If you saw me wandering in the grocery store with no makeup on, my hair pulled back in a ponytail, glasses perched on my nose, with a baseball cap on, wearing sweatpants and a sweatshirt, is that going to be the picture or the image you have of me? If that's how you meet me, is that going to fit your expectation of who I am?

If someone from an online dating service doesn't look like their picture, what does that really mean? One assumes that people want to show themselves at their best on an online dating service. So they're going to put up their absolute best possible photos because it's how *they* see themselves. How wonderful if the picture they present is the best picture of them—because *that* is how they see themselves.

I recently learned something new about this topic. Did you know we can never really see ourselves as we are, or as others see us? We only see ourselves in mirrors, or in pictures. And then we filter those reflections though our beliefs about ourselves. It's been said that if we could see ourselves the way others see us, we wouldn't even recognize ourselves!

Our expectations are what keep us from having what we truly want. I want you to understand this. This is very, very important. When you have an expectation, it's going to get in the way of what you really want.

Let's revisit the online dating scenario: You may have developed an expectation about your date based on what they wrote, or what their picture looks like even before meeting him or her. You may also have an expectation about how a relationship is supposed to unfold in your mind because it's simply how _you_ expect a relationship to unfold. This doesn't necessarily mean that the person you are interacting with is going to meet your expectations—because both of you may have completely different expectations of a relationship. You need to be able to talk about the expectations each of you may have.

For example, what if you have an expectation there has to be an immediate spark between you and this other person? What if, when the person walks into the room there was absolutely no spark, no connection? Do you consider the date "over" at that point? Your expectation may be causing you to miss a lifelong opportunity to be with your soulmate.

I once knew a woman who was set up on a blind date. After that first date she concluded "there was no spark, there was no chemistry." They did have many things in common and began hanging out as friends. Six months later, they looked at each other one day and realized they did indeed have a spark. They had fallen in love. As of today, they've been together for over thirty years.

You need to let go of the expectation that there has to be an immediate spark, or you're going to run the risk of missing the right and perfect mate.

Ask yourself, "What usually turns me off about a person as a potential mate? What is turning me off about my current mate?" If what turns you off is that there is no immediate chemistry, or having nothing in common, you have to ask yourself what that is really about.

Let's say you walk into a room and you see two people. One you may be attracted to and one you're not. The one you are attracted to may be better looking to you. It may be a chemical thing or an attribute from your past. The person may remind you of someone you saw as kind and loving. Or perhaps the "instant attraction" may be part of a destructive pattern that your ego finds attractive. Be willing to explore this honestly. This instant attraction, where you throw all caution to the wind, is often a warning signal. Make a conscious decision to slow down if you find yourself immediately attracted in a "hot and heavy" way.

It's time to set an intention to counteract the expectations. Here's a good basic intention to hold:

> *I see myself being easily and effortlessly with the right and perfect mate. I see myself comfortable with the level of chemistry that occurs between us with each and every interaction.*

This way you won't have an expectation of what the chemistry level and the "spark" are supposed to be. Simply affirm, and set the intention. Sometimes that attraction has to build. You need to give it time to do that. This intention can be helpful:

> *I see myself easily and effortlessly reserving judgment about the true level of chemistry between us.*

Give the Universe a little time to work. Often, the judgments we make are just something from our past that we're bringing into the present. See your judgments as a reminder that this is a new person in your life; recognize that this is *not* the old person you had a relationship with in the past. Otherwise, whenever you're building a new relationship, it's never going to be just the two of you. It's never going to be just you and this new person. It's going to be a triangle. It's going to be the two of you *and* the person from your old relationship, trying to make a go of it in a new relationship.

Turn Your Expectations into Expectancies

What would it take for you to have a fun evening with someone, just simply enjoying yourself without any expectation about where it all may be going? Ask yourself, "Am I staying present, or am I subconsciously looking at this person with an end in mind? Am I picturing this person as the person I'm going to grow old with? Am

I picturing this person as someone who will let me down in some way?"

Take all your expectations out of the equation. Instead, ask yourself, "Can I fully and completely just enjoy being present in *this* moment without any expectation of where this is going to lead?"

I'm not saying let go of all your ideas and dreams for the future. What I'm talking about is letting go of your *expectations*. Have an *expectancy* instead.

An *expectation* is a predetermined judgment about something. An *expectancy* is something you are looking forward to. It's like a pregnancy. You might not know if you're having a girl or a boy, but you have an expectancy that it's going to be a child you love.

It's like Christmas versus a trip to the dentist. Before your dentist visit, you might have an *expectation* that it is going to hurt, or that it's going to be uncomfortable at the very least. With Christmas, you don't know what you're going to get, but you have an *expectancy* that what you receive will be something fabulous.

This person that you're dating, that you have your first date with, is like getting a Christmas present that wasn't on your list. You're trying to figure out what it is and how you can best enjoy it, instead of getting upset that it wasn't what you expected it to be.

If you think this person is not right for you, then you can ponder, "Hmmm... I wonder who this gift *will* be right for?"

Receiving your greatest desires requires you to face your fears. And often the thought of getting what you really, really want can actually cause you to shut down. Oddly enough, it can be pretty terrifying to get what you want.

Maybe a long time has passed since you've been romantically interested in someone. Maybe you felt hurt very badly in the past and that's caused you to shut down. You don't know whether or not you can trust your judgment.

If you've had time between relationships, or stretches of disconnect in your current relationship, ask yourself, "Have you enjoyed your independence? Are you ready to create a change in your life?"

Having a long spell of independence, without an intimate connection is like having had a career and then deciding to change your career. You don't know what the future holds. You don't know what this new career is going to look like; you've never had this career before. You never had this new relationship before.

You are stepping completely outside of your comfort zone into something that is new and exciting—and also extremely scary, all at the same time.

Ask yourself, "What's my biggest fear? What's the worst thing that can happen if I open up to someone?"

It may be that they won't want you. How would that feel? Maybe you would feel rejected, maybe you would feel unworthy. Maybe you would feel abandoned. These are unhealed core beliefs you have—which you can work to dissolve and heal.

Have you ever been approached by someone who *you* weren't interested in? How did you handle that? Were you kind? If you're a kind person, can you assume that, if you're interested in someone and they are not interested in you, they will also be kind and will do their best to not make you feel rejected?

If you've ever stayed in any type of relationship with someone because you didn't want to hurt their feelings, I want you to make a commitment right now. Commit from this day forward that if you go on a date with someone and you know it doesn't feel right to you, that you'll simply say to the person, "You seem like a very nice person *and* this isn't going to go anywhere."

Be kind and do not string the person along with excuses. Be straightforward. You'll soon find that other people are more inclined to be direct with you as well. We receive from the universe whatever we put out into it.

Can you assume that it is not any other person's intention to make you feel bad? Can you assume that if the attraction is not mutual then there is someone *even better* out there for you just around the corner? When you hang onto someone, you restrict that flow. But when you release your attachment to a person, it makes room for your highest good to come to you.

Slow Down So You Can Notice Any Deal-Breakers

Maybe in the past, you have thrown yourself into a new relationship, immediately sleeping with a person after only a date or two. Or if you're in an existing relationship where there has been a break in your intimacy, you may believe you can fix everything by simply jumping into bed together. People sense desperation. You may not even know it is there, but it creates an unhealthy balance.

From now on, as you're creating that right and perfect relationship, that right and perfect mate, hold this intention:

I see myself open and receptive to enjoying the company of this person in this moment, releasing all expectations and attempts to create a relationship.

You're just enjoying the company of this person, in this moment. Take it nice and easy, take it nice and slow and allow a relationship to build at its own pace.

When I do relationship workshops, I always share what I call "The 90-Day Rule." People are often a bit shocked when I describe The Rule (maybe because I'm a minister).

Here is "The 90-Day Rule of Dating": No fingers touching wet skin for ninety days. What I mean by that is, don't get intimate physically with a person for ninety days. And this includes "sexting" in case you were wondering.

All too often, people jump into a sexual relationship so quickly that their hormones take over. They create an emotional and physical attachment to someone without ever really checking in to see if the person is actually a good fit for them.

A woman came to me once, deeply distraught over the ending of a recent relationship. She told me she was more upset about this ending than she had been when her decades old relationship had ended. I asked how long she and this new person had been together. She replied, "six weeks."

What she was really mourning was her loss of the *expectations* she had for this new relationship.

Another woman ignored my advice to wait before sleeping with the man she had started dating. When she broke up with him, after a few months, his response was (a very heartfelt), "I felt cheap and used."

He had an expectation that her sleeping with him meant something about their relationship—whereas she had seen it as just an opportunity for casual sex with a guy she liked. She reached out to get a copy of *Manifest the Perfect Mate* after that incident!

When we wait patiently, we are engaging in the longtime ritual of courtship. Courtship gives us the opportunity to enjoy the attraction *and* get to know a person on a deeper level. By keeping a "level" head as it were, both parties can more easily communicate what they truly want, need and desire in their lives—and determine if those areas fully match up.

We also get a clear-headed opportunity to recognize what I call "deal-breakers" before the line of intimacy is crossed and can't be uncrossed.

Using The 90-Day Rule, you can more often develop life-long friendships with people who you might otherwise wind up ghosting (suddenly and completely ignoring without explanation) or resenting.

A woman recently shared with me that if she had known about The 90-Day Rule years ago, she could have avoided getting entangled with someone who declared early on, "I love hiking!" Turns out, what the other person meant was more along the lines of "I loved hiking in my twenties" rather than a current desire to have an active hiking life.

A few years ago I led a workshop series called *Romanticom*, which was designed to help us laugh at our dating foibles while learning some new healthy relationship skills.

One question I asked shocked the audience. I gave everyone an index card and told them to write down the number of people they had been intimate with. Then I had them write down how many of these people they had slept with for the first time while completely sober and not under the influence of any drugs or alcohol.

Guess how many had "zero" as their second number? Every single one.

This is the benefit of "The 90-Day Rule." Instead of choosing immediate intimacy, I encourage you to change your destiny. Start by having authentic conversations, and let the connection between you grow organically—slowly and steadily blossoming and revealing its true beauty. To help, you might set the intention that:

> *I see myself open and receptive to enjoying the company of a good mate. I see myself comfortably and*

slowly building the right and perfect relationship
with the right and perfect mate.

You can even use The 90-Day Rule for any current relationship you're in. Mutually agree to do a 90-day reset, where intimacy is more of a courtship. Things like a foot rub or backrub that don't lead to anything else. Snuggling without any expectation. Walking each other to your bedroom and kissing each other good night at the door. Even if you're then getting into the same bed together, you can use The 90-Day Rule to revitalize your connection with each other, without having the expectation of sex creating tension.

Now, what if you slip up and don't follow the rule? Sometimes, it may seem like 90 days is a long time. The point of the rule is to keep you focused on exploration, making sure there are no deal-breakers *before* you get intimate. If one night, in the heat of the moment, you go beyond the boundaries you've set with each other, you can always reset the clock.

If you feel pressured (or are the one pressuring) to take it to the intimate level, however, ask yourself why you're not honoring yourself (or your partner) in this process. The ultimate goal is to honor the relationship, the connection between the two of you. Think long-term. If you're dating someone who pushes the bound-aries on this, imagine where else they might push boundaries.

When my beloved and I started dating, I was extra leery about taking things to a more intimate level, since there was a young child in the mix. We both agreed to The 90-Day Rule. We had lots of long snuggles and make-out sessions, for sure. And a ton of time spent just getting to know one another, exploring who we were individu-ally as well as together.

I still clearly remember the day I looked up from the kitchen table and realized "this is the one." It was day 48. The 90-Day Rule had done its work, and our relationship is still healthy and vibrant all these years later.

Erase Any Remaining Fears and Doubts

What other fear still comes up? That having this right and perfect mate won't happen? Why not?

Maybe you see yourself as being a handful, for example. If you're strong willed, it may take someone who is extremely secure to be in a relationship with you. If so, you might want to set an intention such as:

> I see myself attracting to me the right and perfect mate
> who is fully and completely confident and secure in

all areas of their life. I see my mate ready, willing and able to handle me—because I can be a handful.

One of my coaching clients in California manifested a fabulous relationship. One of her criteria as their relationship began moving forward was that they go to therapy *together* to be free from all past relationship issues. They took action together to create this reality.

They had only been dating for six months, but they went to therapy together to work through all their past relationship issues so they could build the long-term relationship they desired.

One big issue that often gets in the way of manifesting the right and perfect mate, as I said from the beginning, is an attachment to past relationship issues. If you're ready to manifest the right and perfect mate, you have to be ready to let go of the past.

This includes past issues you've had with your parents and with anyone you've ever had any kind of relationship with—whether it was romantic or otherwise.

Ask yourself honestly, "What past things am I still hanging onto?"

Do you have trouble believing that people are emotionally available, free from past relationship issues? Try this intention:

I believe that people are who they say they are, and that they are as available as I am.

Write this down on your list of attributes you desire in the right and perfect mate. They have to be emotionally, physically and mentally available—as do *you*.

7

Learn to Stop
Trusting People

⸺ ••• ⸺

A dear friend of mine once said something that I treasure to this day. She said, "Don't trust people—love people. Trust God."

Love people. Trust God.

What does that mean? It means trust the process. Trust the unfolding. Trust that when our ego doesn't get what it wants, there is something bigger at work; there's some inner intuition or whatever you want to call it that *knows* something isn't quite right with what is going on.

If you are trying to put your trust in people, they are always going to disappoint you because "trust" is always based on our personal expectations. If you simply *love* people, they will reflect that love back to you. You give people the opportunity to love.

When we get emotionally tight and don't trust, what we're really saying is, "I'm not open enough to love this person. I'm not willing to take a risk because I'm afraid I'm going to get hurt again."

If you decide to just love that person and take care of yourself without having to protect yourself (don't defend, just take care of or honor yourself), then what you're doing is creating the space for that love to grow. Trust that God (or the Universe) is constantly working for your highest good.

This is what was happening with the woman from Chapter 3, who held sacred space for her relationship when she discovered her husband was having an affair. She did what she wanted to do every night without making him "wrong."

Anytime you feel like you're not trusting the process in a relationship, anytime you start to feel that tightness, that sense of wanting to close up, or pick up your ball and go home—whether it's in a romantic relationship, a work relationship, a friendship, or a family relationship—I want you to do an exercise.

Your gut will know if this is a person who truly isn't ready to be truthful and honest or if they are momentarily in a place of fear. Open yourself up so you can feel the deeper truth; do some "muscle-testing" if you like. Don't open yourself up and then immediately shut yourself down and say, "See, I told you that wasn't the right thing to do! I should never trust people!" The first part of that declaration may or may not be true. The second part, however, is absolutely true.

Exercise: Take a huge deep breath and fling your arms wide out to your sides as far as they can go. You're completely open and vulnerable. There's no way for you to defend yourself because your arms are so far out. Do that. See how that feels. Feel that openness? Feel that tightness in your chest as you realize that you're completely and utterly vulnerable?

In this safe space of vulnerability, you have an opportunity to explore any fear from your past, any unhealed wound, any expectation or projection of a repeated pattern that may be getting in the way of you having a positive, loving connection with another person. Let your breath out in a big whoosh, or slowly, as you desire.

Take another deep breath, and in your mind, send love to any person you're feeling tightness with. Send peace to that person you're not "trusting" 100%. Then give yourself permission to release whatever projection, attachment or past issue that is clouding your vision. Ask your Higher Self to reveal the true nature and the true issue with this person and you. Take another deep breath and ask yourself, "Does this exercise ease this tightness?"

I believe you should never "trust" anyone. Don't trust people. Don't trust *anybody*. Love them instead. It's not about trusting people. Trust God, trust the Universe. Trust that there is a Higher plan and that it is all unfolding the way it is supposed to. Trust that any relationship—even if it exists for just a few dates—is there to help you evolve into the next step in your evolution to make yourself open and ready for the right and perfect relationship that is coming down the road. It could be just around the corner. Not every event in your life is leading you directly to where you are going. There may be a detour you have to take.

If you've ever played a video game, it's a perfect example to demonstrate the path of finding the right and perfect mate sometimes. You don't just go straight from Point A to Point B, collect your gold coins, rescue the princess and call it a day.

You have to go from Point A through the land of the enchanted forest, to get the magical key that takes you across the desert, to open up the portal that takes you into the castle from underground. And you have to go up sixteen flights of stairs, and battle all the monsters, and get through the locked door.

It is a circuitous route to get to where you want to go. It's a route that leads you to where you pick up the tools along the way to create what you want. That's what you've done with relationships in the past and that's what you will want to do with your current mate, or anyone you meet in the future as you're manifesting the right and perfect mate.

If this person you're with right now—or the next person you date—is not the right and perfect mate, it's only because you're there to get a tool from them that you can use when the right and perfect mate does show up. Instead of shutting down and maybe chastising this new person for *not* being who you wanted them to be (hello expectation!), find the good. Find the gift. And move on. It's all about changing your perspective.

Too Old For What?

What other fears are coming up for you about finding the right and perfect mate? Maybe you think, "I'm too old." You're too old for who? Too old for what? How old would you like your right and perfect mate to be?

How would you feel if you're sixty-five and some forty-five-year-old decides they really like you in a romantic way? What fears would that bring up for you? What if you already had a child that age? Would you be bothered by that? How could you possibly be too old if someone twenty years younger than you is attracted to you?

Remember: Once you begin to love yourself truly and completely, that will pretty much take care of the fear of "I'm too old" even if you fall in love with someone who is significantly younger than you. In which case, that's what you truly want. And there's nothing wrong with that, as long as you're both of legal age of consent.

Know When You're Ready for Your Mate

Are you ready to attract someone? Right now? If so, instead of bemoaning the fact that there hasn't been someone in your life, ask yourself: Have I been ready to attract someone during this period, or have I been doing my own growth that I needed to do?

It's time to release any and all guilt about not having found someone. Any and all anger, fear and disappointment. You weren't supposed to find someone during this time. During the time you've been alone, you've been in a relationship with yourself. How well did you treat yourself?

You've been in a relationship. It was the right and perfect relationship for you at that time in your life. Now you're ready to move on to having that relationship with someone else in your life. Every time you start to think,

"I haven't attracted someone so far," stop yourself. From now on, set an intention:

> *I see myself attracting to me an abundance of people I am attracted to. I see myself effortlessly drawing them to me. I see them everywhere I go, and I am open and receptive to allowing them to be in my life. I see myself ready, willing and able to open myself up to a loving relationship.*
>
> *I am opening myself up to love myself. I see myself opening myself up to allowing someone else to love me. I see myself open and receptive to loving them. I see myself open and ready and willing and able to take that risk. I see myself letting go of the past. I see myself releasing all my fears about how and when the right and perfect mate is going to manifest.*
>
> *I know and believe that everything I truly desire in a relationship is coming to me now. I see myself as good enough, attractive enough and loving enough. I see myself secure enough. I see myself able to stay an independent person in a relationship, always meeting my own needs every day, in every way. I love myself fully and completely, exactly as I am.*

Now it's time to do an exercise to keep you fully present to yourself, regardless of your current relationship status. The truth is, you are currently in the most important relationship of your life.

You're currently in a relationship with *yourself*. Your assignment is to see how good of a mate you can be to yourself. How can you demonstrate that you are a good partner and show others how to treat you?

Exercise: Find a ring or another piece of jewelry, but preferably a ring, with no past association to any other person to whom you've been romantically linked. It might be something from the past, from a grandparent, for example. Or it might be something new that you've bought yourself. Put it on your hand, as if you are now in a relationship—as if you are now engaged to yourself.

Wear this ring for six months. Date yourself exclusively for six months. Treat yourself as if you are in a committed, long-term relationship—with yourself.

How well do you treat yourself—your beloved—in this relationship? Do you take someone's number if they offer it to you because you think they're cute? Do you flirt with others or ignore plans you've already made with yourself because someone cute asks if you're available at that same time? How often do you honor the needs you have? How often do you do what it is *you* want to do, instead of negating your needs and desires, and saying "never mind, it's not that important" or "I'm not going to do it, because there's no one else to do it with."

This exercise is so important, I'm going to risk repeating myself. *Be in a relationship with yourself for six months.* Honor that relationship. Treat that relationship like it's the most important thing in the world, and watch what happens.

Stay Present to What Is

Now I want to talk with you about staying present when you are in relationship with someone else, or beginning to date.

Every time a new relationship opportunity comes along, you may feel "this could be the one" or maybe you don't even think about moving forward, fearful of being disappointed if the person turns out *not* to be "the one." Maybe it feels too overwhelming to stay fully present to this moment when you're completely wrapped up in the excitement of the unknown, of the potential.

All this mind madness means we are projecting instead of remaining present. In a situation such as this, I encourage you to use this intention:

I see myself patiently and joyfully allowing the right and perfect relationship to unfold in my life now. I see every person I date contributing to the manifestation of the right and perfect relationship. I see myself enjoying this moment of getting to know this person, fully and completely. I see myself enjoying getting to know this person, released from all expectations about what each moment together means. I see myself fully and firmly staying in the present now.

All too often, when we begin dating someone, we start to project, "If this is the right and perfect person then . . . I see our house, our beautiful yard, and the dog and happily ever after and I start planning the wedding and naming the children (or the dogs!) . . ." As you can see, it's easy to get caught up in that projection, that fairy-tale happily ever after story—because it's what you want.

Stop yourself when you start doing this projecting. Focus instead on seeing the relationship unfolding for the highest good of all. Let go of the *form* you think the relationship is supposed to take. Concentrate instead on the *essence* of the relationship.

I know a woman who spent many years trying to get pregnant. She had a very difficult time and had many miscarriages. She finally gave birth to a daughter. Then, she and her husband tried again and they lost that child before it was born. It was very devastating to her because she had this attachment to wanting a house full of children. She had forgotten that there were many ways for her to have children. They could adopt. They could be foster parents.

Sometimes we have an attachment to the form our life is supposed to take, when all along there's a bigger plan out there trying to draw those people to us. But we're so busy concentrating on what we don't have, and what has been lost, that we miss the opportunity entirely. So watch for that.

Embrace the Constant Presence of Change

News flash: People change in relationships. You won't be the same person you were when your relationship began, even a year later. If you're revitalizing a current relationship, approach the relationship as if you're meeting this person for the first time. Who are they now? Who are you now? What "agreements" have you set up as patterns in your relationship that no longer serve you? What do you want to be doing differently?

A fellow minister once shared a story about the early years of his marriage, in the 1950s. His wife worked a second-shift job but would get up early each morning to make him breakfast (like a good wife would), before he headed off to seminary classes. He would dutifully sit down and eat the meal she prepared.

One morning, he finally got up the courage to tell her he would prefer not to eat breakfast. Relieved, she shared that she would prefer not getting up early to make breakfast!

If they hadn't been willing to communicate what they both truly desired, they could have easily set themselves up for a pattern of resentment.

In my own life, I didn't even realize the pattern I'd created of doing everything "all by myself." I'd been single and dating for nearly twelve years before my beloved and I met. I was in the habit of taking care of everything in my world, around my house, all the time. One evening, about six months after moving in together, I announced that I was too tired to cook dinner. My beloved was overjoyed, "Finally! Now *I* can cook!"

Abandonment: The Biggest Self-Sabotaging Belief

We've talked a great deal so far about various self-sabotaging fears and beliefs. Now, it's time to tackle the biggest self-sabotaging belief in the world: *abandonment*. Abandonment issues are so strong—and so insidious—that many people don't recognize how their tentacles have enmeshed and choked off a relationship until the relationship is gasping its last breaths. Abandonment issues are a huge cause of many unexpected derailments of what could have been a beautiful friendship, if not a beautiful relationship, from the very beginning.

Think about all the times you felt abandoned, left alone, left behind, had your opinion dismissed, felt disrespected. How quickly can you see the scenarios of these stories, with all their vivid details? Those are all projections of the laundry list of people you believe have abandoned you.

Now, I want you to stop and answer one deep question: Throughout the course of your life, who has actually abandoned you the most? If the answer isn't immediately evident, I suggest you look in the mirror.

If you're ready to heal your abandonment issues, it's time to take the first step. Let go of the story of what has happened in the past regarding your relationships. It's time to write a new story. It's time to write a new ending, and a new beginning. Become willing to release your old perceptions—it's all about perceptions, remember? Become willing to release your old perceptions so you can make room for what you truly desire in your life.

Become willing to explore and heal and forgive yourself for all the times you abandoned yourself.

Exercise: Sit quietly somewhere you won't be disturbed. The bathtub works beautifully, as does the forest or the beach or your car. Allow yourself to think of the most powerful memory you have of being abandoned. Feel the whole story, feel all the feelings. Sob your guts out. And when that starts to subside, ask yourself, "What if *that's* not why I feel abandoned?"

Your ego will be glad to provide you with another possibility of *why* you feel abandoned. Allow that memory to wash over you. Repeat the process again and again until you can't come up with any more stories. Breathe. Breathe. Breathe. And then give yourself permission to sleep!

Cultivate Clear Communication

Sometimes, there is value to having a dialogue, or a discussion when abandonment issues are triggered. I talked earlier about the woman who would sit in front of the fire, night after night while her husband was stepping out.

Maybe she was totally oblivious as to why her beloved decided to start a relationship with another woman. Maybe she had a horrible habit that triggered something in her partner that had never been mentioned. Having a constructive positive conversation might have revealed things that could have been worked on or transformed. Maybe there was a way for them to talk and rebuild their relationship together, like the couple who consciously chose to go to therapy.

If you're having a problem distinguishing between when it is valuable to talk about things together and when you can do the solo work of seeing your relationship the way you want it to be, I have another exercise for you.

Exercise: Think back to a time in a relationship where one of you wanted to go into therapy or do something to better the relationship, or have clearer communication, and the other one of you didn't. The best solution for something like that is not to constantly nag and pick and poke and deliver ultimatums. Instead, focus on visualizing the two of you going to therapy together. Or seeing the two of you communicating with compassion, together. Envision what that would have felt like, what conversations you would have had, with your newfound knowledge and self-love.

As you do the exercise, remember: Whatever you see in your mind is what you truly believe. You might not need to know what it was that drove a wedge between you and your beloved. You may *think* you need to know this, you may want to pursue that because you want to know whether or not it was a valid reason (in your mind). But that's just a form of wanting to be *right* instead of *happy*.

Let go of your attachment to the reason things in your relationship changed. Your only question to ask yourself is, "Do I want to be in a relationship with this person?"

You might say, "Well, no, because I don't trust them!"

That's not the real answer.

Do you *want* to be in a relationship with this person?

"I *would* want to be in a relationship with this person if I could trust them." Still not the real answer. Whatever happened occurred because something was lacking in your relationship with each other. Make your question about what each of you want and need in your lives. See if their answer matches up with what *you* want in your life. Then look for ways you both can bridge that gap— if that's what you desire—and find the middle ground where the win-win resides.

There are two exercises that can help.

I'm not talking about being manipulative or being passive-aggressive, and just letting things go on in ways that don't resonate with you. I'm talking about releasing your attachment to wanting to be right. Ask yourself, "Am I engaged in this story because I want them to admit that they were wrong, and I want them to admit that I'm right, and come around to my side, to my way of thinking? Or am I engaged in this story because I'm telling them simply what it is I want in a relationship, and how I'm feeling and what I feel I'm lacking?" It's never about the other person.

Exercise: Start setting the intention in your action and in your mind of what you truly want. And the next thing you know, your partner will bring up the idea of whatever it is you want to create in your relationship.

Exercise: When a partner/spouse becomes agitated in your relationship, start sending them love (including yourself). Start seeing them at peace. Start seeing them released from the need to defend their position. Simply see them as safe and loved, even in the midst of the argument. Release and let go of the attachment to wanting to be right.

"Why" Doesn't Matter

When the woman sat in front of the fireplace and focused on what *she* wanted, she changed *her* behavior. The result was that her husband's behavior shifted. By focusing on what she wanted, the energy shift made it possible for both of them to change their stuck patterns. They may have very well had conversations about why he had an extramarital relationship. But this wasn't what she was focused on. Her primary concern wasn't to get the answer to *why*. When you ask *why*, you're trying to create in your mind a defense, or enough evidence to make it okay.

"I can change something about myself, and then things will be okay." Or "I can understand why he did this and come to a place of peace."

The *why* doesn't matter. The *why* isn't what you really want. When you say, "I want to know *why*," you may get information about *why*—but you still won't have the relationship you want.

Because the *why* isn't what you really want.

You don't really want an explanation; you want a whole, healed relationship.

So ask yourself, "Can I make the conscious commitment to let go of the need to know *why*?"

Holding space and consistently seeing someone as loving and communicative will bring up lots of emotions because it's part of the healing process. It's like ripples coming back to you. You drop this big stone in the water that is your intention and *boom*. It sends the ripples out and they go out and then they come back and you have to deal with them. The ripples go out and they come back, each time coming back with less strength. Each time, they take longer and longer to come back until the water around you—your life around you, the essence around you—is perfectly calm.

But sometimes we don't like calm and we decide to toss in a handful of pebbles to stir things up a bit. Our ego begins to argue that, "I'm not getting *my* needs met," in order to distract you, instead of staying focused on what you really want.

Look at the couple who experienced infidelity. If he had been open to being communicative and working on the problem, then therapy may have been the way to go. But instead of confronting, pushing, and nagging, and further damaging their relationship, she chose to hold the consciousness of what she wanted.

She, too, could have stepped out, and declared, "Fine, if he's going to do *that*, then I'm going to do *this*!" But it wouldn't have created what she wanted: her relationship healed. Instead of focusing on what *he* was or wasn't doing, and taking her attention and all of her energy off of what her desires were, she stayed focused on what *she* desired instead.

If you're having a challenge wrapping your mind around this concept, think of a magician. The magician will be talking to you, gesturing and doing something to draw your attention to the left of the stage, when all the time he's doing something else with his right hand that's creating the illusion you're about to see. He's getting you to focus your attention to the left, creating a distraction.

Think about when you were a child and you were with other children—perhaps siblings or neighborhood kids—and you all got into trouble. Maybe one of the children was being called to task. A child's first instinct is to point out what someone else had been doing, to draw the focus away from them. That's what you do when you try and focus on the thing externally that's gone on, instead of focusing on what you really want.

This woman asked herself, "Do I want a divorce?"

Ask yourself, if you have an infidelity in your relationship, do you want to call it quits? Or do you want a loving relationship with your beloved?

This woman decided she wanted her husband back in his easy chair reading with her like he used to. She just concentrated on that. No matter how many times he went out, she didn't let her mind stray to wondering what he was doing. She focused on what *she* wanted.

A friend of mine used a slightly different technique in her relationship. Her husband often stopped at the bar with colleagues after work, instead of coming straight home for dinner. After one too many homecooked meals got prepared and went uneaten, she decided she had two options:

She could either rant and rave about it, or she could start cooking dinner only for herself and let him make his own dinner when he got home.

She chose to honor herself in her relationship, regardless of what her husband did or didn't do.

Stay the Course

Too often we get so close to getting what we want and then we sabotage our results.

Remember what happened with the woman whose husband was dating a co-worker? She's holding her intention and taking her actions, and suddenly he stays home one night; and then the next night he's gone again.

Instead of her going ballistic on him, which would be an instinctive reaction, to jump into an attitude of "oh, no you didn't! You stayed home last night, and now all of a sudden you're gone again to your girlfriend? This is not going to work for me!" she stayed focused on what it was she wanted.

Instead of executing a deep swan dive into victimhood, blame, shame or withholding, she stayed singularly focused on "what do I want?"

Despite any appearances to the contrary, she used the evidence of him staying home *one night* as proof of the progress she was making, instead of seeing it as a setback.

Focusing on what you want can seem challenging. It's almost as if we are culturally inclined to focus on what we *don't* want. And maybe what you want *isn't* to stay in the relationship.

I once worked with a woman who discovered her husband not only had a girlfriend—he had taken the girlfriend on a Valentine's Day trip, after canceling a trip he'd arranged with his wife. The affair was revealed when the hotel accidentally called to verify "her and her husband's dinner reservation."

Rather than go ballistic, she calmly asked herself what she wanted. Once she had clarity, she sat down and typed up a separation agreement outlining what assets she wanted from the marriage. When he arrived home, she announced she knew about his latest infidelity, that she was no longer interested in being with him, and that he was going to sign the separation agreement and get out of the house, for good. Which he did.

The woman in our first story wanted her husband home. And he stayed home that one night. So she decided to keep focusing on what she wanted, because she knew he was going to come home. The woman in this last story wanted her husband gone. And she stayed focused on what she wanted, despite the sadness and anger she was experiencing.

8

Rewrite the Story of Happily Ever After

Sometimes, as I outlined at the end of Chapter 7, "happily ever after" doesn't look like it does in the fairy tale. Sometimes, it looks very, very different.

Years ago, I stopped by to see my friend Janet. Her daughter and granddaughter were visiting. Her granddaughter likes dressing up as a princess, and Janet had bought her these pink plastic princess shoes. One of the shoes had broken, so Janet told her granddaughter she could play Cinderella. Her granddaughter didn't understand who Cinderella was and what that meant. I explained to her that she had to go around and place the shoe on everyone to see whose foot it fit.

After trying the shoe on all the adults, she realized that the shoe only fit her. She slipped the shoe on and I said, "Look, you're Cinderella! Now Prince Charming is going to come and swoop you up and you'll live happily ever after."

There was dead silence in the room. Janet and her daughter and I just sat there. Then Janet sighed and said, "But that's not always how it works, is it?"

So we chose to rewrite the story for her grand-daughter.

We examined how often we tell the "happily ever after" story to our children and grandchildren without rewriting the story first.

As a result, when they get into a relationship they think it's always supposed to be happily ever after, everybody looking out for each other all the time, never a down day, never anyone snapping or cranky or what-ever. Never someone *not* saying, "I love you."

We forget to teach people, especially our own chil-dren, that they can just allow their loved ones to be. We forget to share that loving someone doesn't change just because they have a habit that *we* find annoying, or just because we're mad at them in the moment or because one of our core beliefs got triggered. That you don't run away and shut down. You just step away and take time to care for yourself—and give the other person time to do the same. Putting yourself in "time out" is a powerful action for creating healthy, peaceful, loving relationships.

A couple I know in New Jersey is an excellent example. They've been married for decades, and have four amazing (now grown) children. They once told me a story that happened when they were engaged. They were driving to see the minister and talk about their wedding.

They got into an argument on the way to the church and the wife-to-be got out of the car and refused to get back in the car with her husband-to-be. They were several miles away from the church and he went ahead to the appointment so he wouldn't be late.

When he showed up, the minister asked, "Where's your fiancé?"

The man replied, "We had a fight on our way here, she got out of the car and she wouldn't get back in."

The minister said, "Let's go get her."

So they got in the car together, drove back, and pulled up next to her. When the minister asked her to get in the car she said, "I'm not getting in the car with *him*!"

The minister asked, "Well, does this mean the wedding's off?"

She looked at the minister like he was insane and said, "*No*, it doesn't mean the wedding's off, it just means I'm not getting in the car with him *today*."

When you're mad, that doesn't mean a relationship is ending. It just means you happen to be mad that day. The same goes for whomever you are dating.

If you give people room to be themselves and allow them to have their feelings, and not try and fix the situation, and not close down because *they're* shutting down—you open up a huge opportunity to create the relationship you really want. When you focus on what you *don't* want, you close the door on any such opportunity.

The fear is that if you honor yourself, speak your truth, or stand up for yourself, then the other person will leave you, or stop dating you, or stop calling you. That's the fear.

Have you ever stood up for yourself where someone *didn't* leave, even once?

If so, focus on *that* as a reminder. That's how mature, supportive, secure people react. If you're dating someone and they do leave because you expressed your feelings, then say, "Thank you!" because they weren't the right and perfect mate for you. But you learned how to stand up for yourself, how to honor yourself.

You want someone who is secure enough to understand that if you're angry or shutting down or not getting in the car, all that is actually happening is that you are honoring yourself—which has nothing to do with them.

Of course, you want to learn how to express your anger in a respectful way—and there are ways to do that which are kind and compassionate. You don't have to rant and rave at them. You can just say, "Hey, look, I don't want to talk to you right now. I'm mad as all get out at you and I'm not speaking to you."

Country star Terri Clark recorded a song called "I Just Wanna Be Mad." It made it to the number one slot on the country chart because it tapped into this essence, this truth. The song brought to light the realization that it's okay to be upset at something and it *doesn't* mean you're ending the relationship.

> *I'll never leave, I'll never stray*
> *My love for you will never change*
> *But I ain't ready to make up*
> *We'll get around to that*
> *I think I'm right, I think you're wrong*
> *I'll probably give in before long*
> *Please don't make me smile*
> *I just wanna be mad for a while*

Being okay with your authentic feelings just means you reserve the right to honor your feelings to be mad for a while. It's okay to feel your feelings and work through them.

Agree to Disagree

Some people have a strong expectation of what communication looks like. I remember once visiting friends—a

longtime lesbian couple—who I "adopted" as my "moms."
One partner was Sicilian and the other was Irish. Two
passionate women, and their communication style
reflected this passion.

The first time I witnessed them having a "heated
discussion," I suddenly found that I had moved onto the
veranda and had made myself as small as possible. I'd
been raised in a German household where it was rare to
have people yelling at each other.

They eventually found me—and explained they
were not arguing at all. They were simply having a conversation. Loudly. Which then made perfect sense to me.

Certain ethnic groups talk passionately. About
everything. Yet for others, someone raising their voice
sets off a "danger, Will Robinson" signal. The raised voice
represents anger, not passion.

Someone who doesn't have a cultural expectation
that arguing is a part of communicating is going to get
scared. Because inside they're taking it seriously; they're
taking it personally.

A woman I know who is Jewish seemed really angry
at her husband one night when I was a dinner guest. She
yelled at him for about fifteen minutes, then she looked
at him and calmly asked, "So, what do you want for dessert?" The conversation was over. In her mind there
hadn't been an argument, she had simply said what she

needed to say and he understood that. It was just a conversation style they had agreed on.

You may need to make an agreement about the conversation style in your relationship. Maybe you agree not to yell at each other. Particularly if you came from a home where people yelled and belittled each other. You have to identify your own agreements. Creating the relationship you really want means being willing to take the risk that the person you're with may not agree. What you want in your relationship may be a deal-breaker for the other person.

These agreements and decisions and your ideas for yourself and your life may not mesh with theirs. They may leave. But if you use honest, clear communication, you may reach a resolution. Let's say you're used to having a diverse range of friends and your beloved was raised in a less diverse environment. You have to be willing to say, "These are my friends, these are the ideas I have about people, how do you feel about that?"

If you've got gay friends, black friends, Hispanic friends, and you're dating someone who is racist or homophobic, is that going to be the right and perfect relationship for you if suddenly you feel uncomfortable hanging out with your friends? You need to ask yourself these hard questions. If you're conservative, and your beloved is liberal—like the Matalin-Carville household— can you agree to disagree, or agree to not talk politics at home? The choice is yours.

If you're thinking about compromising on a "deal-breaker" because you are afraid of never finding a mate, you need to release the fear that you're always going to be alone. People cling to relationships sometimes because they're so afraid of being alone. When you start creating the relationship that you want with yourself, doing the things you want to do, even when you're not in a relationship, you eradicate this fear. The fear disappears because you're honoring yourself. You're saying, "This is who I truly am in a relationship." You're not changing who you are to meet your perception of another person's expectation.

When you start stepping up, when you start having a true relationship with yourself, you begin to know you're already complete, with or without someone else. Then anyone who comes into your life is someone who will complement you, not complete you. When you release this fear and start creating the life you want for yourself, then you no longer fear them leaving. Their presence or absence no longer means anything *about you.*

Yes, you may miss them if they're gone. You may mourn them. You may cry your eyes out for a while. But then you pick yourself up and you dust yourself off and you say, "There was a great gift for me in that relationship, and I may or may not see it right now, but I'm ready to move on and do what I need to do for me."

I am open and receptive to someone coming into my life, and I'm comfortable enjoying them in this now moment.

Honor Your Differences

You may want to do different things than your mate or potential mate might want to do. That's okay. Honor the things *you* want to do and let them honor the things *they* want to do. Find common ground activities you can do together, and release any expectation that just because you do something *they* want to do, that means they're going to do the same thing for you. If you're doing something to spend time with someone rather than because it's something you really enjoy doing, you're doing a grave disservice to your relationship.

Stop it! Stop abandoning yourself and start honoring yourself. Tell your beloved, "Go have a great time at NASCAR. Go have a great time at the symphony. I don't like racing—*to me* it's dirty, it's noisy. I don't like the symphony—*to me* it's depressing, it's boring, it's stodgy." Whatever. Just honor that. Allow yourself to be separate people who complement each other. Work on allowing things to just be what they are in the moment.

One couple I knew had vastly different tastes in movies. Finding a film to agree on often meant one person wasn't entirely thrilled with their date night entertainment. They developed a brilliant solution. I share it with you here to help you imagine possible solutions for your own life.

The couple would find a theater playing two movies beginning and ending at approximately the same time, so they each would have an exciting movie option. They went out together for a nice dinner. After dinner they walked down to the movie theater, and bought a single ticket for the movie each wanted to see. They kissed each other, and went into their separate movies. When they came out, they went somewhere nearby for dessert and shared information about their movies. Brilliant!

A woman I know drives out to the beach in Rehoboth, Delaware often. On one trip, she encountered a very interesting man at a bookstore. They decided to have dinner together, and hung out all evening talking. They had a delightful time, but she'll probably never, ever see the guy again. It was just a lovely evening. She didn't try and make it into more than that. She just allowed it to be a lovely evening.

Work on allowing things to just be what they are in the moment. Whether you're dealing with a long-term relationship or a first date. Just allow each encounter to be a lovely moment and you'll be amazed at how much freer you feel—and how much less anxiety you will feel about being alone in your life.

Your old story may have actually been "they *didn't* live happily ever after," or the resigned, "it is what it is," followed by a deep sigh.

Armed with the tools in this book, your new story is that you are complete, whole and enough. Let the past stories about your life dissolve. Release them. Allow the element of surprise to reside in the midst of your relationship.

At a Saturday workshop in Maryland, I gave out the assignment that for three weeks people could only tell positive stories about their lives, including the past. One long-married couple commented that, "It's going to be *really* quiet at our house for the next twenty-one days!" And then the funniest thing happened when they arrived at church the next morning.

They looked like newlyweds; they were glowing, laughing and holding hands.

They couldn't wait to share what had happened. The husband blurted out, "We've learned more about each other in the last twenty-four hours than we have in twenty-four years of marriage!"

9

Allow Your Relationships to Just Be

<figure>⸺ ... ⸺</figure>

Imagine what a change in perspective could do for you and your present or future relationship. It's all about allowing "what is" to just be. In this final chapter, I want to expand on the concept of "allowing." Here are some tools you can use to step back and allow things to unfold.

Be, Just Be
Practice just being. I once told a woman to, "Just be," and she loudly replied, "It's on my to-do list!" Just be. Breathe in. Breath out. Smile. Lather, rinse, repeat.

Be Honest
Be willing to be 100% honest about how you feel.

Don't be afraid to say, "Hey, I'm really enjoying our evening here, and I'm starting to feel a little uncomfortable because I kind of like you. That scares me because in the past I've been known to jump into relationships too quickly—and I don't want to do that again."

Actually say it.

I once met a woman who said she wanted an open, honest, communicative relationship, but she was afraid to ever speak up. If you want a relationship that is open, honest and communicative, it starts with you. It starts with you, with each and every encounter.

Share your truth. Open up a dialogue with the other person. Put your fear out on the table and you drain its power.

Fear is like a germ; fear is like a little bacterium. It cannot live very long once it's exposed to open air. But it will sit there, and it will fester forever if you leave it inside you. If you leave it in the dark, it will grow and multiply and have a grand old time and it will destroy any chance at love. Because the only way you can love is to be open.

Be Patient

Check in to see where you still have internal work to do to make sure you're ready to have someone else in your life. And release your attachment to the *form* that relationship takes.

My favorite story that illustrates this is from a woman who attended a workshop and wrote that she wanted a man who loved her company, loved doing the things she was passionate about, and loved her unconditionally.

What happened? She got an unexpected grandson; who loved her company, couldn't take his eyes off her, and loved going with her and doing all the things she loved doing. She quickly realized that *this* was indeed the right and perfect relationship for her! She released all expectation of what she *thought* she wanted and made room for her heart's desires to appear.

If you don't want to wait, if you want it now, and you are prepared to *be* that right and perfect partner, then you *can* have what you desire now if you've done all this inner work.

Do you truly believe that tomorrow you could meet someone who loves you *as you*? If you truly believe it, then there is no reason for you to have to wait. But if you say it and then you think, "But I'm afraid that I'll repeat the same pattern; I'm afraid I'll jump into something and it won't be a healthy relationship," it means that you really don't believe it or that you're not ready for it.

To believe something means that you know it completely. Just like you know beyond the shadow of a doubt that Christmas comes on December 25, you know that the right and perfect mate is in your life right now in some form, in some shape, and that this relationship will unfold and be revealed to you in divine timing.

Richard Bach, the author of *Illusions*, tells a wonderful story in one of his books about how he was having an out-of-body dream where he was bemoaning the fact that he couldn't find the right and perfect mate. An inner voice filled his head very loud and very clear. "You have already met her, Richard. You already know her."

It freaked him out and he started going through his list of women he knew, and he couldn't figure it out. A while later, he met a woman, an incredible woman, and they began hanging out as friends. Then one day he realized—they *had* met before.

They had met more than a decade before. He was getting off an elevator going to his accountant's office and she was getting on the elevator. They passed, glanced at each other, they might have even exchanged pleasantries. It was an incredibly short encounter, but they had actually met each other.

And later she became his wife.

He wasn't ready at the time they met to have a long-term relationship with her. He had to become more of his true self. When we have a loving relationship with ourselves, other loving relationships simply emerge from the crowd.

Manifesting the right and perfect mate doesn't have to be *difficult*. It just simply is *different*.

Now, with the tools you've gathered from this book, you have a different way to approach your relationships. I wish you the best of luck in manifesting the right and perfect mate in your life. To guide you on your way, I leave you with one more intention.

I see you open and receptive to drawing the right and perfect mate to you and having the patience and the courage to work through your relationship issues.

Be sure to send me your intentions. And be sure to send me a card or letter or pictures of you and the people you're dating. And, of course, be sure to send me an invitation to your wedding.

Resources

André, Rae. *Positive Solitude: A Practical Program for Mastering Loneliness and Achieving Self-Fulfillment.* New York: HarperCollins, 1991.

Hendrix, Harville. *Getting the Love You Want.* New York: Owl Books, Henry Holt and Company, 1988.

Hendrix, Harville. *Keeping the Love You Find.* New York: Pocket Books, Simon & Schuster, 1992.

Howe, Carol. *Healing Relationships (documentary video).* Denver: New Thought Classics, 2018.

Ponder, Catherine. *Open Your Mind to Receive.* California: DeVorss & Company, 2008.

Smith, Manuel J. *When I Say NO I Feel Guilty.* New York: PenguinRandomHouse, 1985.

About The Author

Paula Langguth Ryan is an internationally renowned communications facilitator, conflict resolution consultant and speaker, specializing in helping people recognize and resolve conflicts in all areas of their lives with compassion and clarity. Her daily *Conflict Free Zone* radio aired worldwide for two years and her *Manifest the Right and Perfect Mate* and *Break the Debt Cycle—for Good!* workshops have helped transform thousands of lives.

As a communication facilitator, Ryan has worked with individuals, couples, families, small groups and large communities in ten countries to create positive outcomes using her "Ryan's Rules of Order" as a guideline for sustainable success in a multitude of diverse settings.

Ryan is the author of *The Art of Tithing, Bounce Back From Bankruptcy* and co-author of *Effortless Freedom from Clutter and Debt*. She has been featured extensively in national print, radio and television outlets.

Ryan lives in Colorado with her beloved, her son and their Irish Wolfhound, where they all practice these principles on a daily basis—even when egos would prefer otherwise!

Visit her website for more details and information.

www.paulalangguthryan.com

Thanks for reading! Please add a short review on Amazon and let me know what you thought!

CPSIA information can be obtained
at www.ICGtesting.com
Printed in the USA
JSHW020459060521
14392JS00005B/42